DRIVE HER WILD
100 sex tips for men

DRIVE HER WILD
100 sex tips for men

Katy Bevan

Photography by John Freeman

LORENZ BOOKS

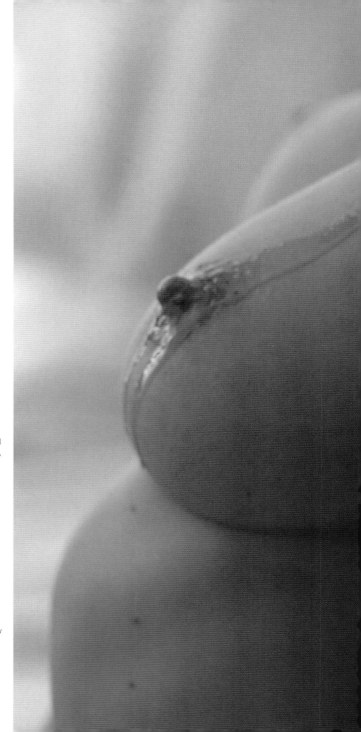

This edition is published by Lorenz Books
Lorenz Books is an imprint of Anness Publishing Ltd
Hermes House, 88-89 Blackfriars Road, London SE1 8HA
Tel 020 7401 2077; Fax 020 7633 9499; www.lorenzbooks.com; info@anness.com

© Anness Publishing Ltd 2004

UK agent: The Manning Partnership Ltd,
tel. 01225 478444; fax 01225 478440; sales@manning-partnership.co.uk
UK distributor: Grantham Book Services Ltd
tel. 01476 541080; fax 01476 541061; orders@gbs.tbs-ltd.co.uk
North American agent/distributor: National Book Network
tel. 301 459 3366; fax 301 429 5746; www.nbnbooks.com
Australian agent: Pan Macmillan Australia
tel. 1300 135 113; fax 1300 135 103; customer.service@macmillan.com.au
New Zealand agent/distributor: David Bateman Ltd
tel. (09) 415 7664; fax (09) 415 8892

A CIP catalogue record for this book is available from the British Library.

Publisher – Joanna Lorenz
Managing Editor – Judith Simons
Project Editor – Katy Bevan
Copy Editor – Alison Bolus
Designer – PB Wagon for RB-M Studio
Photography – John Freeman assisted by Alex Dow
Hair and Make-up – Bettina Graham
Production Controller – Pedro Nelson

10 9 8 7 6 5 4 3 2 1

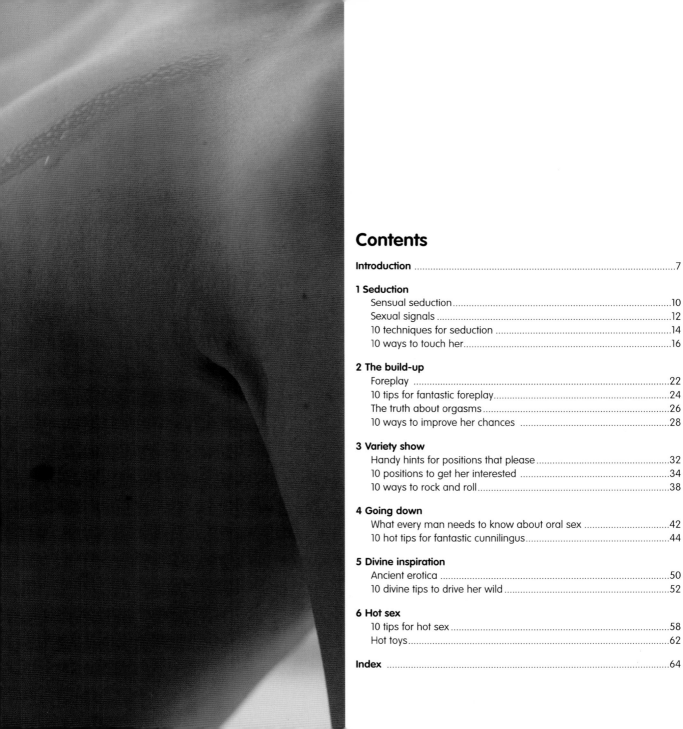

Contents

...a little knowledge of the female anatomy can go a long way to turning you into the greatest lover she has ever known...

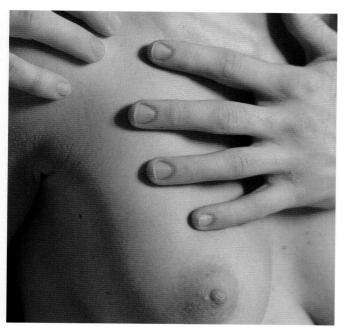

Introduction

You have spent so much time wooing that woman to get her into your life, your flat, and hopefully your bed, that little thought has been given to what to do when you get there. This is a common mistake, and much depends on you overcoming the indecision and plain awkwardness that can ensue. This little book gives you enough good ideas and sound information to keep you in with a chance. If it is the fear of what could happen next that is holding you back – whether you are planning a night of passion or just a relaxing cuddle on the sofa – you will be armed with the knowledge of what she wants.

These days, women want more – they will not be satisfied with the selfish behaviour that men have been getting away with for decades. Women are also more sexually aware than in the past. There is a constant media bombardment about sex, and women are on better terms with their bodies than ever before. Lots of men feel alienated by (even a little afraid of) strong women who know what they want, and wonder if they can ever measure up.

The fact is that what women want is not generally the big performance that men get so anxious about. What they want, in fact, is attention. They need to be listened to and they want you to respond to the signals they are giving out. This may be a new language for some men, so listen up and start learning. A little knowledge of the female anatomy can go a long way to turning you into the greatest lover she has ever known.

If your partner is not enjoying sex, then something is going wrong. Sex should be blissful for both parties, though not necessarily at the same time. Rather than wait for her to buy herself a vibrator, why not choose one for her, or casually steer her into a sex shop one day? But don't make the mistake of thinking that sex is all about gadgets and positions; it is to do with mood, atmosphere and how your day has been. It's true: the brain really is the biggest sex organ.

1 Seduction

...There is nothing more attractive than meeting a man who smells fresh and clean...

Sensual seduction

It is all in the anticipation – the longer the build-up to sex, the better the crescendo when you finally arrive. That is true for you, as well as her. While men can be aroused by looks alone, women tend to be affected by all the senses at once, that's all six of them, so keep on your toes if you want to get lucky.

How you look is important to her, so don't skimp on the grooming. Clean fingernails are a must – she will be imagining where they are going to go. If you are particularly hirsute, take care – scratchy facial hair not only gives women stubble-rash but can also be a bit of a turn-off. Check other areas like your eyebrows. Hairs between the eyebrows can make a face appear severe, unapproachable – a pair of tweezers can solve this quickly, and put you back in the running.

Your teeth are important, as they will be checked out by anyone thinking of kissing you. If your teeth are stained from smoking or drinking coffee, then invest in some tooth whitener. Make sure your breath is inviting – bad breath is the ultimate turn-off.

Getting fresh

Finally, make sure you smell nice. Have a shower before you go out, especially if it has been a hot day. There is nothing more attractive than meeting a man who smells fresh and clean, although the musk of natural body scents have proved to be a big turn-on as relationships progress. Don't make the mistake of dousing cologne all over your body, as this will mask your own unique aroma. No one can be sure if people really do fall for a particular individual purely because of their scents and smells, but have you ever heard a woman say, "It's not that he's particularly attractive, there's just something about him..."?

Women love to be kissed, and kissing can set the pace for the type of lovemaking you both want to indulge in. Try a slow, loving kiss, caressing her mouth with your tongue, or a more passionate,

frenzied kiss where you are slightly rougher and more urgent with each other. Small kisses all over your lover's body will make her go wild with desire.

A survey carried out on kissing showed that women like kissing more than men and enjoy the whole long, lingering embrace, without it necessarily leading to anything else. In fact, some women have said that they find kissing the most erotic part of sex and have often had an orgasm just from a passionate session of kissing.

Go on a kissing tour of her body, rather than confining yourself to her lips. The best way to find out where her erogenous zones are is to work your way around her whole body. Start at one end and don't be distracted until you have made a comprehensive trip. You will learn a thing or two, and she will think you are the world's best lover.

Sexual signals

Most people have a radar that tells them when another person is interested, but some people are hard to read. This is when an understanding of body language is invaluable. Women tend to use body language more than men, but many signs are used by both sexes. Men are, however, notoriously bad at reading the signs, so a bit of study into what each gesture really means is crucial to getting ahead in the dating game.

You should start reading body language even before the first approach. When talking to a woman, watch how she sits, how she looks at you, and be aware of even the smallest gestures, because they all mean something. Body language, such as someone looking coy and touching their lips or chin with their fingers is a sure sign that he or she is attracted to you. Another positive indication that the attraction is mutual is when you feel comfortable casually touching one another or just being close.

If the woman you are interested in displays at least four positive signals, you may be in luck – it is not a form of consent, but it means you might stand a chance. If you notice that you are, in fact, getting the opposite of these signs, it's time to stop talking and start walking so as not to waste your valuable time on a lost cause. You don't care; they weren't your type anyway, right.

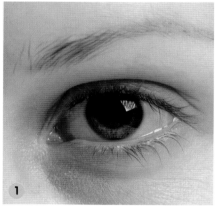

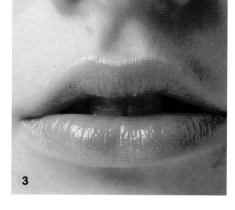

1 Eye contact
The way we catch people's eyes is usually momentary, so if a woman gazes at you for longer than the regulation three seconds, she may be interested in you. Look out for dilating pupils (the black bit of the eye getting bigger) – this is a dead give-away. She may be blinking more than usual. If she is really coy, she may look away and look back through fluttering eyelashes.

2 Where to look
Once you have started holding eye contact with her, it gets interesting. You may find that you don't know where to look next, but your brain has already decided. When talking to a woman in whom they are interested, men will automatically start making a triangle with their eyes, looking from eye to eye, then down to the mouth. Gradually the triangle will get larger to include her chest. You may find her gaze checking you out lower down.

3 Mouth moves
Staring at the mouth is a sign that she may be wondering what it would be like to kiss you. Give-away signs are biting her lips, wetting her lips and showing her tongue, touching the front teeth. If you want to create a good impression, just smile.

4 Matching and mirroring

You may find yourselves mirroring each other's movements. As you lean back to sip on a drink, she does the same. This can be used consciously and is a great way to put the person you are talking to at ease, as it says you are interested. You may also find that she matches her voice to yours, speeding up and slowing down when you do and imitating your speech patterns.

5 Directions

If you are interested in a woman, you can direct your whole body towards her. You may find that your feet are already subconsciously pointing that way. This is a classic indication of interest, so look to see if she is doing it too. She may also be leaning forwards across the table and decreasing your personal space. This is a good sign. Watch out if she starts to lean backwards, especially if she crosses her arms or gazes up at the ceiling. What did you say?

6 Hand contact

If she touches your arm, thigh or hand while talking, you are making a good impression. Lovers will constantly make almost imperceptible contact with each other. If you are touching each other at all, to punctuate the conversation, or even to pick some fluff from your jacket, then you have already moved from the mere acquaintance corner.

7 Fiddling about

Women tend to draw attention to their bodies by fidgeting. She may be fondling keys or stroking a glass or bottle. Best is twirling her hair around her fingers. Perhaps she is imagining what it would feel like to be stroking your hair, and you can bet that thought has already crossed your mind.

8 All fingers and thumbs

Hands are also good indicators of intention. If she is exposing the palm of the hand while facing you, or cupping an elbow in one hand and holding the other hand out, palm up, this shows an openness to contact. Hands down means you're out of luck

9 Blushing

It's an old one, but true. Most of us have experienced unwanted blushing on meeting someone we like. Chances are that the other person won't notice, but if you do happen to notice her skin tones reddening slightly, particularly on the face and neck, you'll know how she's feeling, won't you?

10 Do you come here often?

Forget about those witty one-liners. You will probably have decided whether you like each other in the first four minutes of meeting for the first time. By the time any words have passed your lips, it may be too late. However, be aware that the tone and intonation of your voice are important. If you are feeling tongue-tied, ask an open question and let her do the talking.

13

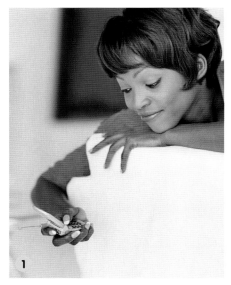

1

10 techniques for seduction

Once you are through the basic looking stage, there are various things you can do to prove yourself as king in the art of seduction. Romancing your lady-love at a distance, by phone or by mail, or by sending her flowers, is a sure-fire way of keeping her interest up when you can't be together. When you are together, make sure she knows just how wonderful you think she is, before letting that innocent flirtation develop into some more indulgent French kissing.

1 Hot text

Use text messaging as a form of foreplay, with suggestive and provocative messages to keep your partner on the boil, or simmering, before you meet. On Valentine's Day it is estimated that over 4 million messages are sent, most of them far too raunchy to repeat here. Men and women report that they feel more confident texting than talking face to face, probably because it has a form of anonymity about it.

2 Who calls who?

If you are a phone person, a call the next day after a date is good, either to say thank you or to make sure they got home safely – both reasons are fairly innocuous and won't compromise you. If you want to play it cool, leave it for a couple of days before you pick up the phone, but not too long – by being too cool you may well freeze yourself right out of the picture. There is nothing so tragic as a relationship that never gets off the ground because you haven't phoned because she hasn't phoned, and she hasn't called because you haven't phoned her.

3 Red letters

A card or letter is always a good bet. It is so exciting to receive a plump, small, hand-written envelope through the post. It's much more personal than a text message, and you have the added advantage of the sensuality of the whole experience – opening the envelope, feeling the paper, analysing the handwriting – plus you can re-read it as many times as you like. If you are not gifted with prose, a postcard is good, and you can let the picture do the talking.

2

4 Gifts

The post is still a great medium to use in courtship. Chocolates, sweets, a book – none of these costs too much to send by post. She will love receiving a gift, because she'll know that you've been thinking about her and have taken the time and trouble to find something that you think she will like. Sometimes an inexpensive gift is more thoughtful than one that costs loads of money. As they say, it's the thought that counts. So if you can't afford a box of chocolates, send a bar – but preferably a good one.

5 Say it with flowers

Flowers are one of the traditional symbols of romance. It may seem old-fashioned to send a bouquet, but most women will go weak at the knees when presented with some beautiful blooms. A red rose sent to her workplace could produce a few blushes, as well as some comments from her colleagues, and it will work wonders for her reputation. A droopy bunch of carnations from the petrol-station may not have the same effect.

6 Opening gambit

Some of the most successful lines are simple, inoffensive openers, such as, "Do you want to dance?" or "Can I buy you lunch?" The least successful lines are those that are smug or flippant, such as, "You remind me of a woman I used to date", or "Bet I can out-drink you!" Remember that what you are trying to do is gain her attention and present yourself as someone with whom she might have a relationship – even if it lasts only as long as the dance or meal itself. Once you've gained her attention, the world is your oyster.

7 Attention seeking

She will think that the sexiest thing in the world is your undivided attention. This woman is the most fascinating you have ever met, and she needs to feel like it. Concentrate on personal attributes rather than material ones – compliment her beautiful smile, not just her earrings.

8 Flirting

The most important thing to remember is that flirting is usually innocent and light-hearted. Try to avoid going into any situation with the thought that "this could be the one" at the back of your mind, as this could make you anxious from the start. Keep relaxed and cool about it – at the end of the day she is usually just another person looking for love. Enjoy the excitement of meeting a totally new person, keep an open mind and have fun.

9 French kissing

Relax your mouth a little and gently caress the inside of your partner's mouth with your tongue. As she responds, you can quicken the pace and intensity, going for a fuller thrust. Be aware of her reactions so you can modify your behaviour accordingly. She may find light chicken kisses all over her face and neck particularly exciting.

10 Talking

It is not polite to stare. If you are out with a woman, you are obliged to enter into conversation. Eventually. You never know, it might actually be interesting. This is an opportunity to get to know her, and to tell her a little about yourself. Try to resist telling her at length about your amateur sporting career, unless she expresses a genuine interest. Likewise, it might be politic to steer away from anything you feel too strongly about, so that you don't get carried away – once you get on that soapbox you may never see her again.

10 ways to touch her

We all need to have some human contact to keep us sane. Research has shown that the art of massage and touch has therapeutic effects on people both physically and emotionally. Children, for example, who were starved of touch and physical contact often display antisocial behaviour, and the absence of touch and caress in adult life can lead to a loss of vitality. Women love to be touched with affection, not just when you are making a move, but out of friendship too. You might be surprised how much she will be affected by simply stroking her skin. Try not to dive straight between her legs, but explore other parts of her body – fingers, toes, armpits and belly button – first. Really tantalize her with massaging hand strokes and tender licks and kisses.

The skin is the largest organ that feeds the brain with information on our external environment. If the skin is caressed in a loving, gentle manner, then the brain will also relax and unwind. When preparing for seduction it is very important to set the scene. Being massaged in a fully lit room with blaring rock music may appeal to some, but for true sensuality it is better to dim the lights or even use candles, scent the air with essential oils and put on some soft relaxing background music.

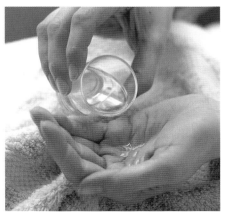

1 Circle strokes

The circle stroke stretches out the muscles, releasing tension from the soft tissues. It is best applied to any broad surfaces, such as the back, thighs, chest or stomach. To begin, place both hands on the body, flat and side-by-side. Lead with your right hand and begin to move them in a circular direction clockwise, using a constant pressure. The aim is to keep both hands adjacent to each other at opposite sides of the circle, so that your right hand will have to pass over the left. Lift your right hand to allow the left to pass underneath before gently replacing it and continuing the sequence.

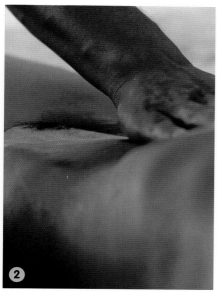

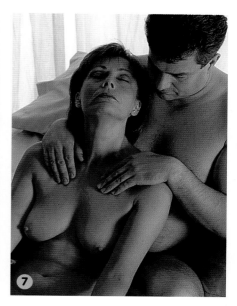

2 Fanning strokes

As with the circle stroke, fanning also releases tension from the soft tissue. This is ideal on the back, as it has a large, broad surface. It can be performed either upwards or downwards. To fan upwards, place both hands flat at the base of the spine at each side of the spinal cord. Glide them both up, concentrating pressure in your palm before fanning them out to the sides of the body. From here, mould your hands around the sides of your partner's body and drag them downwards to the base again.

3 Kneading strokes

These are ideal for the fleshy areas such as the buttocks and thighs. It is quite an invigorating stroke, which releases tension from the larger muscles. Imagine that you are kneading dough by squeezing a portion of flesh in your fingers and then rolling it from one hand to the other and back again. Keep your wrists and arms relaxed to ensure that the massage remains fluid and relaxing. Some oil is a good idea so that you don't pinch.

4 Percussion strokes

These are rapid strokes, which induce a vibration-like sensation that can be very arousing. They help to improve skin tone and help with blood circulation to nerve endings. Hacking, which involves a series of chopping movements with alternate hands concentrating on the same area, is one of the most popular percussion strokes. The wrists must remain relaxed so the action is bouncy and not too harsh. Hacking up and down the back, focusing on the spine, induces feelings of great relaxation in the lucky recipient.

5 The navel

The skin around the navel is a lot thinner than elsewhere, making it an extremely sensitive area. Go on a circular kissing tour around her stomach, spiralling in on the navel in the centre. Once it is wet with your kisses, you can blow on it gently, while massaging her abdomen with your hands in a circular motion. She will spend the rest of the evening wondering which woman taught you that move.

6 Foot fetish

Feet are a sensitive subject. If you can get close to her feet without her collapsing in paroxysms of laughter, then a foot massage can be very erotic, while also safe and not too naughty. Try to resist chewing her toenails, however tempting it may seem. The instep of the foot is a sensitive, nerve-rich area that can be licked and stroked. Many people love to have their feet massaged and pampered – according to reflexology, they are a window on the whole body, so you never know what you might be stimulating.

7 Neck and head

The neck is a very soft and vulnerable place, and hence very sexy. Having it stroked makes most women tingle, and kissing it sends them wild. From the nape of the neck to the crook where it joins the shoulder, there is plenty to get your teeth into (though not too literally). The shoulders harbour the stresses of the day, so a shoulder massage, combined with a little neck caressing, is sure to get her more relaxed.

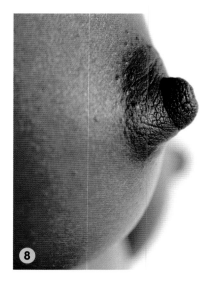

8 Breasts and nipples

Massaging the breasts is a hugely enjoyable process for both of you. Women will enjoy varying amounts of pressure, as breasts can be more or less tender depending on the time of the month. They may also prefer to start by having their breasts touched lightly, with the pressure increasing as the arousal intensifies. The nipples become erect when aroused, and respond well to stimulation – either by finger, tongue, or surprise her with an ice cube. Some women find breast stimulation so erotic that they won't be able to stand it for long – they'll be begging you to move on to the next stage of lovemaking.

9 Legs and thighs

The large muscles of the legs and thighs can use some serious pummelling. Compared to the nipples and breasts, the skin and tissue of the legs are much tougher, so put some effort into it: she wants to feel rejuvenated and stimulated – not tickled. Lift her legs, one at a time, and support the foot with your shoulder, while massaging the upper thigh with the palms of your warmed hands. You might want to use some oil to make the whole experience more sensual. Use your kneading strokes to reduce her to putty in your hands. Alternatively, use one hand to support her leg and the other for the massage.

10 Lips

Now you have worked your way up and down her body and arrived at that most delicious point: a plump set of ruby lips. Begin by tracing the contours of her mouth with your fingers. Then do it again, but this time ask her to lick your fingers first, so that you moisten her lips as you go. Now move on to nibbling her lower lip, then the upper lip – gently teasing her with tiny, whisper-like bites interspersed with some slightly firmer ones. Make a trail of kisses all over her face, before finally returning to her lips and seducing her with a luscious kiss. Now she is all yours…

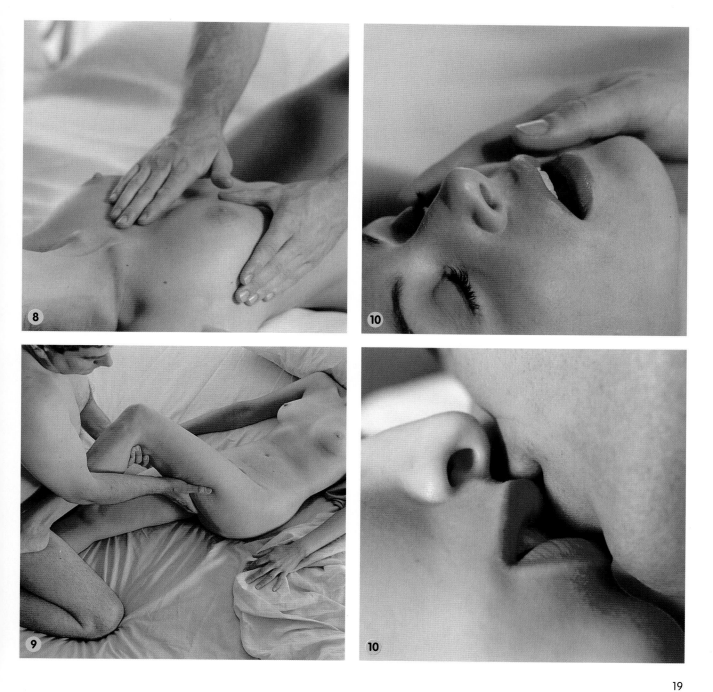

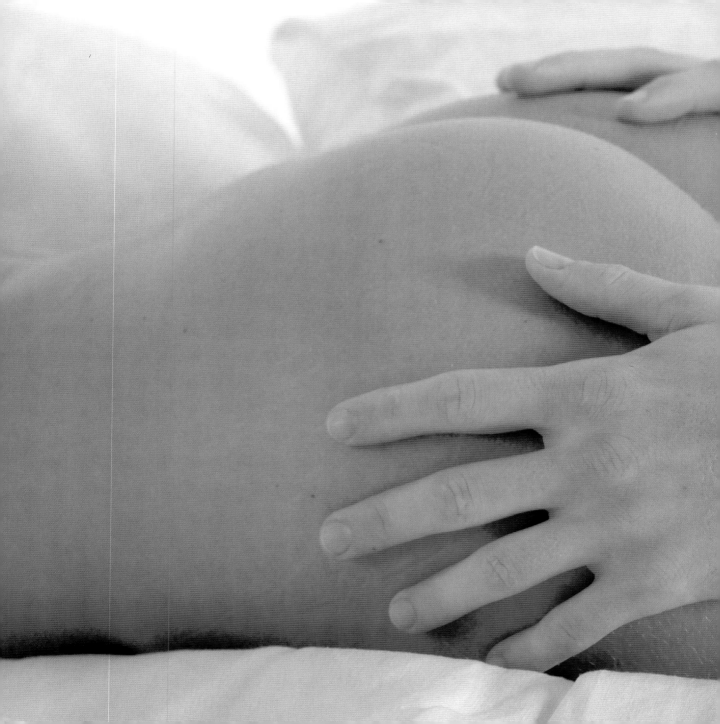

2 The build-up

...foreplay can be the most exciting part of sex, so prolong it for as long as possible...

Foreplay

Foreplay should not just be a means to an end, but something that is enjoyed for the pleasure it gives in its own right. This includes emotional foreplay as well as sexual. Touching, undressing and kissing are just as important as your finger action. While men tend to regard foreplay as something to be raced through before getting on to the serious business, women feel differently about it. They go for the whole ambience thing – lights, music, atmosphere, gentle caresses and so on. Get it right and the object of your desire will be putty in your hands. Get it wrong, and you'll be outside in the rain.

Foreplay can be the most exciting part of sex, so prolong it for as long as possible. If you're feeling cheeky, put some music on and treat your partner to a long, slow, sexy striptease. It's also erotic to remove each other's clothes – take your time, unbuttoning one garment at a time and savouring each one. You'll be working each other up into a lather of anticipation of what's to come.

The nitty-gritty

For many women, clitoral stimulation is the only means of getting sexual fulfilment and orgasm, and it is thought that a woman is three times more likely to orgasm this way than through penetrative sex. The geography of the female genitalia can be a source of much confusion and frustration to men, so an improved understanding of how everything works and where it is located will greatly improve your technique and the satisfaction of your partner.

The vulva is the visible outside part of the female genitalia. The protective folds, or lips, that make up the vulva are called the labia, and these are rich in nerve endings. The clitoris varies in size and shape from woman to woman, but it is always located just below the pubic bone, so it can be gently manipulated and stimulated through intercourse (depending on the sexual position). The head is only about the size of a pea but it has 6–8,000 nerve endings, which is why some women find direct stimulation too intense. Under the hood, the erectile tissue that makes up the rest of the clitoris forks off towards the back of the pelvis. The surrounding protective clitoral muscles are also extremely sensitive, and their contraction aids a woman's sexual response.

By pulling back the clitoral hood, you can clearly see the glans, which is composed of erectile tissue that enlarges during arousal. Under the hood is a flexible cord known as the shaft, which feels rubbery to the touch. The majority of the clitoral structure is inside the body, but the head, or glans, is clearly visible from the outside too. The third part of the clitoris is a wishbone-shaped structure inside the body. In total, the clitoris is about 9cm/3½in long.

1

10 tips for fantastic foreplay

Foreplay is a fine art that involves all the senses to set the mood. Most men could get aroused almost any time, anywhere, with pleasing results, but for women it is often more complex. Preparation beforehand, to get her in the right frame of mind, will pay dividends later. You should be able to tell if you have hit the right spot by her reaction. If you get lost, it's OK to ask for directions – get her to guide your hand into position, and she can show you the kind of pressure she likes. Don't see this as an admission of failure on your part, more a valuable lesson to learn.

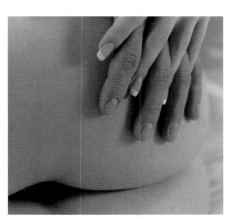

1 Setting the scene
Dim the lights, put the answerphone on and feed the dog, making sure that you give yourselves a window of distraction-free time, unless you are excited by rushing and perhaps the possibility of being discovered. You might consider starting your romancing by sharing a sensuous bath, scented with delicious-smelling rose petals, of course.

2 Exploration
There is no correct or incorrect technique – the important first step is to explore her body and find out what goes where in her pleasure zone. It's also important to experiment with touch and caress to find out what she likes, since preferences vary greatly from woman to woman. Try stroking combined with gentle kisses. These can progress to nibbles, and even gentle bites.

3 Lubrication
Using lubrication can often help to get things moving a bit more smoothly. You can use water-based lubricants, which are usually odourless and tasteless, or even your own saliva. Some women produce more love juices than others, so lubrication is not necessary. Either way, it evokes a different sensation and experience, so experiment.

4 Crossed clitoris caress

Using your third and fourth fingers, caress her clitoris and the surrounding areas in a cross-like movement, moving from north to south and then east to west, with the clitoris as the central point. Change the direction and pressure until you discover her most sensitive spots. Another favourite, which is fairly self-explanatory, is the figure of eight. The top of the eight concentrates on the clitoris and the bottom incorporates the vulva and labia. Use a smaller circle for the clitoris and larger, more sweeping curves for the bottom circle. Use your forefinger and middle finger for this, or whichever two fingers feel most comfortable.

5 Passion pinching

Gently squeeze her clitoris between your thumb and forefinger or middle finger and lift it slightly, squeezing at the same time. Roll it between your fingers, starting slowly and then picking up momentum. Again, experiment with different paces and pressures. For a women with a super-sensitive

clitoris, this contact may be too intense. If this is the case, try to keep the clitoris covered with a layer of the inner labia, avoiding direct stimulation.

6 Circular cyclone

This is an old favourite that, once perfected, will guarantee orgasm. Place your forefinger and middle finger just over the top of her clitoris and rub over it in a circular motion , varying the size and frequency of the circles. Because you are stimulating just above the clitoris, you can use a bit more pressure. Use lubrication if necessary.

7 Finger magic

Some women like to feel something inside them while they are being stimulated. Try slipping a finger inside her vagina, hooking it towards the front of her pubis. You may feel a rough patch on the front wall: this is her G spot. Rest your finger here, using gentle, still pressure. She may initially feel that she needs to pee, but once over that hurdle she should enjoy it.

8 Tri-digit fidget

This one uses three fingers. Use your fourth finger and forefinger to hold back the inner and outer labia folds, leaving your middle finger free to concentrate on clitoral stimulation. Alternatively, with your middle finger and forefinger in a V shape, rub up and down her vulva with the clitoris in the middle. This stimulates the sides of her clitoris and the inner labia. By varying the width of the V, you will get different reactions.

9 Tapping

Spread her labia to expose the clitoris fully. With your index finger, lightly tap the tip of the clitoris. This is not for everyone, and some women may find this sensation too much, but it adds variety and spice in combination with other techniques.

10 Breasts too

Don't ignore her breasts and nipples. Having these stimulated at the same time as her clitoris can be all it takes to drive some women wild. If you run out of hands, use your mouth.

...For men, it is all fairly straightforward... for women, orgasm is more controversial and complicated...

The truth about orgasms

Although it is said that women are capable of having multiple orgasms, there are also a lot of women out there who are not sure if they have ever had an orgasm at all. For men, it is all fairly straight-forward, and it is usually quite obvious when you have succeeded. For women, orgasm is more controversial and complicated. Freud, for example, while not denying that there was such a thing as a clitoral orgasm, believed that the most satisfying orgasm for a woman was a vaginal one, experienced through penetration by the penis.

But then, how much did Freud really know about women anyway? Since it is estimated that only around thirty per cent of women can have orgasms through intercourse alone, Freud's insistence has made many women who need extra clitoral stimulation to reach a climax, feel a failure in the orgasm department. More recently, sexologists have recognized that when women have orgasms, they are due to clitoral stimulation.

No one wants to be the partner of a woman who has failed to orgasm, but it's not always that easy. She needs to get to know her own body first, to understand what turns her on, and where and how she likes to be touched. Then she can be the expert to instruct you. Don't go thinking you can change her life – she needs to do it herself, although you might be allowed to watch, and even participate if you are lucky.

The science bit

When a woman's clitoris is stimulated and she becomes aroused, (the excitement phase), blood rushes to the pelvic area and her vagina becomes moist. The vagina expands and lengthens, the clitoris and breasts swell and the nipples become erect. In the plateau phase, the vaginal lips puff up further, the walls of part of the vagina swell with blood and the opening to the vagina narrows. The woman's heartbeat

increases, her muscles stiffen and a pink flush may appear over her body. At this point the clitoris sometimes disappears; if the woman's partner is in the middle of stimulation, this can be disconcerting. Just before orgasm, the inner labia (lips) change colour.

At orgasm (the third phase), the muscular tension and engorgement of blood vessels reach a peak. When the orgasm happens the vaginal walls contract rhythmically every second for a few seconds and tension is released. The number and intensity of the contractions vary with the individual. Stimulation of the G spot can induce female ejaculation of a liquid similar to male prostate fluid. The muscles of the uterus also contract at orgasm, pulling up the sperm so that they can find their way to the right place. In the fourth phase, resolution, the genitals return to normal. This phase can last up to half an hour.

10 ways to improve her chances

Many women have infrequent orgasms or no orgasms at all and, over the years, this can take its toll on a relationship. This lack of orgasms doesn't necessarily mean that the couple aren't having good sex, but the dynamics of a woman's arousal are quite complex and it doesn't help that the design and position of the clitoris make stimulation somewhat hit or miss. Many women have difficulty reaching orgasm through penetration alone and need extra stimulation of the clitoris by finger or a vibrator. Pushing your penis or pubic bone against the clitoris when you can, may also help.

1 Coital alignment technique

If your partner doesn't usually achieve orgasm with penetration, try the coital alignment technique (CAT). Start in the normal missionary position but then lift yourself forwards, further up the woman's body, so that your thrusts make contact with her clitoris. She can wrap her legs around yours, keeping her pelvis stretched so that her ankles lie in the vicinity of your calves. Alternatively, she keeps her legs closed while you place your legs on the outside of hers. Try both ways to see which one seems to suit her better. Begin a light rocking motion back and forth, keeping in rhythm with each other.

2 Extended sexual orgasm

ESO is done with the woman lying on her back and her partner between her legs, either kneeling or sitting. As you could be there for anything up to half an hour, choose a comfortable position. Begin by applying lubrication to her entire genital area, massaging everywhere except the clitoris. When she begins to move her body to the rhythm of the massage, begin slow, rhythmic clitoral stimulation, while she flexes her pelvic floor muscles and takes deep breaths. When the first set of orgasmic contractions commences, shift stimulation from the clitoris to the vaginal walls by inserting a couple of fingers, but keeping the rhythm steady and slow. Once she achieves her first orgasm, wait for it to subside slightly, but not so long that the contractions stop. Continue massaging the vaginal walls slowly and rhythmically and if she feels the contractions subsiding, move back to the clitoris, maintaining the momentum. This should trigger further contractions, whereupon you move back to the vaginal wall massage, continuing this back and forth movement until the contractions become continuous. Finally, stimulate both areas at the same time, resulting in wave after wave of continual orgasms.

3 Multiple orgasms

Women are capable of having multiple orgasms, but most don't realize it. Some claim that the second or third is less intense, whereas others claim that intensity builds with each one. The techniques for achieving multiple orgasms in women are similar to those described in ESO, where stimulation after the first orgasm continues. Many women find the clitoris hypersensitive to touch after orgasm, so instead of stimulating the clitoris directly, her partner should stimulate the surrounding areas until feelings of arousal return.

Multiple orgasms come in waves, one after the other. Sequential orgasms come on and off after a few minutes. For both, you simply have to keep stimulating her clitoris. If it is painful to do so after orgasm, which it quite often is, try stroking the vulva area or other parts of the body. Many women enjoy multiple orgasms through masturbating with vibrators, rather than by penetration. Don't get left out, buy her a buzz-toy as a treat and make sure you get to use it too.

4 G spot

The G spot, named after Dr Grafenberg who claimed to have found it in 1950, is located in women on the front wall of the vagina about two inches up. To stimulate this patch, insert a finger into an aroused vagina and press up toward her navel until you feel a small rough patch of skin. If you have a vibrator, buy an attachment that is specially made for G spot stimulation. It's easier, apparently, to have multiple orgasms with G spot stimulation and she may experience a full body sensation. This is also very close to the tissue that surrounds the urethra, so pressing it may induce the urge to pee – so if she makes a hasty exit, you'll know why. Pressing is said to be more effective than rubbing here. There is still some debate about whether the G spot exists at all, though you might enjoy experimenting before making up your own minds.

5 Hunt the sex zone

Every time a new sex book is published, it is heralded by the supposed discovery of another revolutionary new erotic hot spot. Here are the latest two to be "discovered".

The anterior fornix erotic (AFE) zone is on the opposite wall of the vagina to the G spot. Apparently it is bigger, easier to access and more sensitive than the G spot. Apart from manual stimulation, you can use your penis to find the spot.

The U spot is a tiny area of external tissue above the opening of the urethra and right below the clitoris. Any stimulation here needs to be very gentle as a urinary tract infection will put a stop to any fun.

6 Simultaneous orgasm

Simultaneous orgasm is supposedly the ultimate goal of lovemaking. If it happens, then fantastic. However, not many couples manage it, so don't get disappointed. Anyway, there are reasons why it may not be such a good idea. What about watching your partner orgasm? And if both partners are concentrating on their own orgasm, there can be a sense of dislocation in which both feel momentarily separated from the other.

7 Faking it

Okay, so we've all done it. Mostly faking is done to bolster the ego of the other person, so they don't feel that they have failed to satisfy you. But everyone loses in this situation: you won't know that she isn't getting all the stimulation that she needs, and, what's more, she won't get it. If you think your partner is not enjoying sex, buy her a vibrator as a gift. If she can explore her own responses, with or without you, it may help.

8 Women who don't orgasm

For the majority of women who can't orgasm, it is generally for a psychological reason. A number of cultural, social or relationship issues are involved here. Difficulty achieving orgasm can be caused by anxiety, control issues within a relationship, past sexual abuse, or a fear of being penetrated. It can have roots in your religious upbringing, if you have been told that sex is dirty and encouraged to feel guilty and deny yourself sexual enjoyment.

This may seem like a long list of problem areas, but they can be resolved by the right approach from you. Start by discussing any problem with your partner and then, if necessary, see a sex therapist or counsellor.

9 Women who can't orgasm

Some women simply cannot orgasm – a state sometimes referred to as anorgasmia, "the inability of women to achieve orgasm, even with stimulation". It can have a physical cause, such as illnesses, advanced diabetes, or it can occur if a woman is on certain drugs, has hormone deficiencies or anorexia. If you think your partner may have a physical problem, encourage her to get checked out by a gynaecologist if she has decided to do that herself.

10 Play the game

Sex is a bit like a game of snakes and ladders. You can get nearly to the end, then you slip all the way back to the starting post. If your partner is not relaxed, orgasm will not happen for her. Go back to basic seduction, making sure that the atmosphere is conducive, the lighting dimmed, and so on. In some relationships it is destined not to happen at first, so be patient.

3 Variety show

...as far as women are concerned, some positions are more equal than others...

Handy hints for positions that please

The positions assumed during sexual intercourse are key to the amount of enjoyment a woman receives. Most men admit that they would like to satisfy their partners, and the key is clitoral stimulation. There are plenty of positions out there that have equal amounts of joy to bestow; it's just that, as far as women are concerned, some positions are more equal than others. Your average man can get as much pleasure behind the bike sheds as in a romantic situation – but for women it's a different story. Sordid will not do: women like to be in a safe, relaxing and romantic place. That doesn't always have to be in front of a cosy fire in a mountain-side retreat, with the natural smell of pine and no one else for miles, but it helps. Don't try it out on a dirty floor at a party, covered in cigarette butts and sticky beer, unless it is your last two minutes on earth.

Some men are under the misapprehension that women don't enjoy sex. Not true: women just don't like bad sex. There is nothing so disappointing for a woman as meeting a gorgeous hunk of a man and then finding out that he is a Neanderthal in the sack, with no concept of foreplay and a total concentration on pleasing himself. So read on: it will be time well spent.

Don't get into the routine of always doing one position because it is familiar and safe. It won't take long for that to grow stale. Impress your woman with your worldly knowledge and adventurous spirit. You don't have to be Indiana Jones (except for the crack of the whip, maybe) to ring the changes every once in a while. However, while you are dreaming of exotic postures you can get into, make sure you are going to be able to get out of them as well. Be realistic: if you are not gymnasts, then there is no way you are going to feel comfortable performing some of the more demanding positions. Feeling relaxed and at ease is a must, otherwise those elusive orgasms are not going to come out to play.

Extra stimulus

About seventy per cent of women do not orgasm through penetration alone. They need extra stimulus, and that means the clitoris or G spot. Either you have to discover a position that creates some friction on one of her hot spots, or else you need to free up your hands so you can do it manually. You should have worked out by now how she likes to be touched – gently and rhythmically will usually do it.

Slow down: racing to the finishing line won't do any good, especially if she is still under starter's orders. It can take considerably longer for a woman to get up to speed, especially in the initial stages of lovemaking, so give her a chance to keep up. Better still, give her your undivided attention for part of the time, so that she doesn't get left behind in all the excitement.

2 Legs eleven

Kneel on your heels with her legs wrapped around your neck or up on your chest. From here you can lean forward and caress her breasts and nipples. If she has her legs wrapped around your neck, this is perfect for deep thrusting. If her feet are resting on your chest, this will make her vagina feel tighter, as if gently gripping the penis.

Press your hand on her lower abdomen and you may be able to feel your penis as it moves in and out. Gentle pressure here

10 positions to get her interested

There are really only six basic positions – everything else is a variation on a theme. However, in most of them there are some tricks that should steam up her glasses. If you want to try out something very unusual, it might be wise to run it by her first. It takes two to tango, you can't just go imposing some mad ideas without getting her to agree, although once you have wowed her with your intuition (that means you changed the sheets before she came round, aired your room and bought some scented candles) she will be up for anything, within reason. Remember: stimulation, atmosphere, and speed. Keep those three key rules in mind and you will be fine.

1 Missionary monotony

There is something to be said for the familiarity of this old favourite – although the basic man-on-top position has, among women, the reputation of being a good opportunity to catch up on their nail-filing. The main problem with this position is that it is not so good for clitoral stimulation because the penis is often not at the best angle. Try holding her around the waist and lifting her up so that she arches her back, then you can penetrate even deeper.

As you are on top, you are more able to control the rate of your thrust and, therefore, when you come in this position. Slow entry and almost total withdrawal of your penis will drive her mad: place the tip of your penis just inside her vagina, then withdraw it, repeating this slowly or quickly. This creates a wonderful feeling and heightens sexual tension. However, be careful if you are highly aroused, as you may come too soon.

Another plus point is that you can see her face, both as a guide to what excites your partner most and to arouse your own feelings still more. It is, undoubtedly, a very versatile position that can be adapted to all kinds of places if you are feeling adventurous. However, a small woman can be quite squashed by a heavy partner, even if he takes most of his weight on his hands or elbows, so don't try this following a large meal.

stimulates the parts of the clitoris that are inside the body. Also her G spot, on the front wall of the vagina, will be stimulated.

You can easily watch her expressions in this position. Some women will find the deepness of the thrusting painful, and will not be able to tolerate for it for long, so look out for the wince that tells you it's time to stop. If you are of priapic proportions, you must take care – big penises can cause pain if you are thrusting deeply. Having said that, this can be an exciting position for both partners, and great for relatively quick sex.

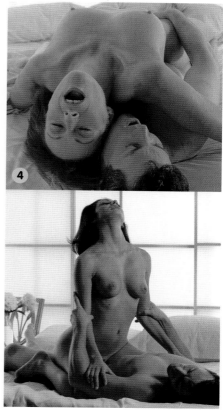

3 Cliff hanger

Surprise your partner as she is sitting on the edge of the bed. Push her (a little rough and tumble is erotic) so that she falls back on to the bed. Lie over her and hold her legs around your neck as you kneel on the floor. Your hands will be occupied, although with the pubis raised up, she may be getting some clitoral friction naturally. (Not every woman's clitoris is in the same position, so you will have to make it up as you go along.) You can watch as she abandons herself to passion. Some women love to have a strong, decisive lover, while others may feel overwhelmed. Watch for her reactions so you can modify your behaviour accordingly.

4 Getting an eyeful

Lie down and encourage your partner to sit on top of you, facing your feet. Enter her as she lowers on to you. Women love to show off this normally concealed, voluptuous part of their body. If the woman leans right back, you can stimulate her clitoris with one hand while holding her with the other. If she sits up slightly, you can contribute to the thrusting with your hips and she can be still. If she leans forwards, then massage her back and buttocks and, if she likes it, place your finger around or into her anus (remember to have the lubrication handy before you begin.) as there are many erotically charged nerves in this area.

5 Women on top

OK, so most men admit to this being one of their favourite positions, but how do you convince her that she will enjoy it too? A woman who is reluctant to take the reins may feel self-conscious about her body. When she is lying down, her stomach is flatteringly flat. The minute she sits up, everything starts wobbling about. What she doesn't realize is that that's what you are looking forward to. Tell her how much you like the way she is. If you are on top, hold her in your arms and roll over so she is almost there. Once she realizes that she has control of her own arousal, as well as yours, this may become her favourite position.

6 Sitting down

The seated positions are very intimate, allowing for lots of kissing and caressing, which women love. The movements are limited, but there is no need to rush, so you can spend time perfecting them. They allow the woman to rock backwards and forwards and so stimulate her clitoris.

Sit up with the woman on top, face-to-face and her legs wrapped around you. If you keep some distance at first, you can stimulate her clitoris and caress her breasts. When you enter her, rock your way to an orgasm.

This is a very easy way to introduce an element of variety. Circular thrusting movements work well here, and these will stimulate the sides of her vagina. This works as well on a chair as on a bed, and is great for hugging, kissing and full body contact.

7

6

7 Spoons

This is a great one for spontaneous sex when you have been sleeping, or just having a cuddle. It is good for a wake-up call, as stale morning breath can be avoided. Neither of you is obliged to do a lot of work here, but there are infinite possibilities for touching, as your hands are free. Since you aren't facing each other, you can happily carry on in your private fantasy world.

Snuggle up behind your partner as she draws up her knees towards her waist, and slot in behind her. This is pure skin-on-skin contact. Kiss her shoulders and neck and nibble her ears, while reaching around to cup her breasts. You can also reach down and stimulate her clitoris or, alternatively, if there is some lubrication handy, place your finger around or into her anus while whispering dirty things in her ear. This position is a useful one to remember after a long night, as it still works if you have only a partial erection.

From the basic side-by-side position, lean back while she leans forwards. Grip her hips and enjoy the deeper penetration. Women often find the sensation of being gripped firmly as penetration deepens very erotic, so this should be a sure-fire way to please her. Spoons don't have all the fun…

8 Up against the wall

Standing positions work better if you are both of a similar size, although you can always use the first one or two steps on the staircase to get the height correct. These positions engender very intimate embraces, because you have total body contact and can kiss and caress each other constantly.

Penetration is not very deep, but this is more than made up for by the incredibly erotic nature of spontaneous sex, not least because it somehow seems a little naughty. Even if there is no danger of someone walking into the room and surprising you both in the throes of passion, you can always pretend that this might happen, to add a little frisson of excitement. (Of course, if you really are having sex where someone could discover you at any moment, then the urgency and excitement will be all the more intense.)

She can put her arms up against the wall or around your neck for balance. If you are leaning against a mirror you will get a full frontal as well. Your hands can grip her hips or buttocks. There's plenty of scope for touching, caressing, nibbling, nuzzling, licking and every kind of body contact.

9 The wheelbarrow

You may remember this position from your school days, when you had wheelbarrow races on sports day, though this version promises to be much more fun. Stand behind your partner, who should be leaning on her elbows on the bed, and hold her legs out straight. Alternatively, you could kneel on the ground, with the woman on her elbows on the floor. Once you have lifted her up by the thighs, pull her on to your penis slowly. You won't be able to do anything else with your hands. Unless you are an athlete, this will be a quick one, with vigorous thrusting. There's not a lot the woman can do except be penetrated and be amazed at your athleticism. Lots of laughs are guaranteed with this one.

10 Doggy style

Being taken from behind can be very arousing for women. Although it can be rather impersonal, that is also part of its attraction. Since you can't see her face, she doesn't have to feel guilty about the fantasies she is having about that film star. Meanwhile, you don't have to worry about the stubble on your chin giving her a rash, so everyone is happy.

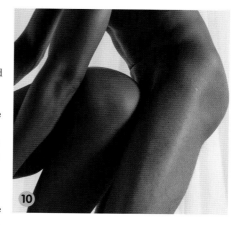

There are several ways to go about rear-entry sex: lying down, standing, or with her bending over doggy-style. With all of these there is the opportunity for using your spare hand to stimulate her clitoris, so increasing the pleasure for her. The natural curve of most penises fits perfectly with the shape of the vagina in this position, so deep penetration is possible here. Although this can be very erotic, there is a danger of hitting her cervix, which can be painful, so be careful.

10 ways to rock and roll

Like they say in the song, it's not what you do, but the way that you do it that gets results. Now that you know all those tricky positions, it's just the start. What matters next is the movement, whether it is thrusting, bumping or grinding.

The *Kama Sutra* has quite a bit to say about how a man should please his woman. It is his duty to make sure that her *yoni*, (the Hindu word for the female genitalia) is satisfied. It is interesting to note that such an ancient text contains views more enlightened than many you can hear today.

1 Going in deep

Deep penetration can be equally enjoyable for both of you. It can stimulate your partner's G spot, if the correct angle is achieved, and you can enjoy the sensation of the tip of your penis coming into contact (gently) with your partner's cervix.

Psychologically, it makes you feel like a well-endowed stud, and she feels that she's so irresistible that you can't control your desire.

2 The tip of the iceberg

Shallow penetration can also be equally gratifying for both parties. For the woman, the opening of the vagina is rich in nerve endings, and for the man, shallow penetration provides constant stimulation of the frenulum and head of the penis, which can be squeezed and stimulated by the muscles at the vaginal opening. Many couples enjoy shallow penetration that involves rocking together back and forth: it is highly stimulating as well as being very relaxing and loving.

3 Finding your level

Partners soon find out what level of thrusting and penetration they prefer, and consequently use positions that best suit them. Equally, they will choose a position

for deep or shallow penetration depending on their particular mood or sense of sexual urgency. If deep penetration is what you and your partner enjoy, use plenty of lubrication to heighten the experience, especially as many women don't secrete enough naturally.

4 Take care

Astonishingly, each year thousands of people are admitted to hospital with injuries sustained while attempting unusual sexual positions. When trying out exciting new positions with your partner, remember to keep within your limitations and bear in mind that although alcohol may remove

inhibitions, it doesn't, sadly, make you any more flexible, more agile, more supple, or any younger. So keep within your physical limits.

5 Please her yoni

The *Kama Sutra* says firmly that it is the man's duty to please his partner. To this end it suggests sensual movements that can increase her enjoyment (such as churning). Grind your penis in circles once inside her, avoiding thrusting movements.

6 Piditaka (pressing and piercing)

Press your penis hard towards her womb and hold before withdrawing and repeating.

To "pierce", penetrate her from above, being sure to come into contact with the clitoris, and pushing against it to arouse her.

7 Varahaghata (the boar's blow)

Provide continuous pressure on one side of her vagina during your initial penetration, before releasing the raging bull within you…

8 Vrishaghata (the bull's blow)

Thrust wildly in every direction while you penetrate her. Don't get too carried away, though, or you might put someone's eye out.

9 Chatakavilasa (sparrow sport)

Quiver your penis while it is inside her, and move lightly in and out. She will think this is divine, which of course it is, sort of.

10 Mix'n'match

For many partners, variety is the spice of life, so be prepared to enjoy everything you've learnt so far in different combinations. A mixture of shallow and deep penetration could drive your partner wild, as you tantalize her with repeated shallow strokes – bringing her nerve endings to screaming point – interspersed with the occasional deep thrust that will take her breath away. As you both reach the point of no return, increase the number and intensity of the deep thrusts.

4 Going down

...there is nothing more sensual and pleasurable than lying back and being orally stimulated by a genital genius...

What every man needs to know about oral sex

The whole issue of oral stimulation for women – going down – is one that sends spasms of fear through many men. How a woman wishes to be stimulated is so individual that it takes a lot of time and communication to get it just right. It is difficult to gauge exactly how to stimulate the clitoris without some help from your partner, and even then it can be tricky, as many women know how to stimulate themselves but often find it difficult to explain and teach. As your relationship progresses and you begin to learn to read each other's bodies, cunnilingus gets better and easier; practice does, after all, make perfect.

The act of oral sex is an extremely intimate and trusting one in which you invariably find yourself opening up to your partner and allowing them access to your most sensitive and private places. In fact, when you think about it subjectively, it is actually quite a bizarre ritual. Licking, sucking, tasting and pleasuring your partner is a very emotional experience that requires commitment, not only to your partner but also to the task in hand.

The techniques used for explosive oral sex are extremely different from those of penetrative sex. By refining the art, you can get a greater understanding of your partner's sexual preferences. It is an exciting journey of exploration into your partner's hot spots – a journey that is equally, if not more, exciting for them.

For many people, the difference between being an average and an exceptional lover lies here: skilful cunnilingus is worthy of an award. For your partner, there is nothing more sensual and pleasurable than lying back and being orally stimulated by a genital genius. Some people worry that the active partner in oral sex is not getting their "fair share". Sexual pleasure and orgasm are not like a bank balance – being "in the red" should be a privilege.

Soixante-neuf

The 69 is tricky. Many people find it hard to concentrate on stimulating as well as being simultaneously stimulated. It can be difficult for you to hit your partner's hot spot in this position, as your chin is stimulating her clitoris. Similarly, it is the less-sensitive top side of your penis that receives most stimulation. Height differences can cause problems, too, making one partner curl and the other stretch.

So why do it? Well, apart from the fact that it is a real giggle, it can also be quite effective. The sight of each other's most private places up so close can prove to be an astonishingly erotic experience. If your partner goes on top, she is more in control and you can lick her dangling breasts. You can massage her buttocks (most men find their partner's bottoms arousing) or just concentrate on her genitals.

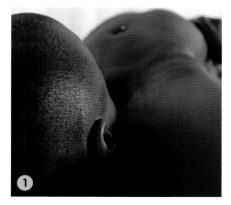

10 hot tips for fantastic cunnilingus

Performing cunnilingus is a luxuriously time-consuming act. Bear in mind that you may be doing it for a while, so make sure that you are both comfortable. The best positions are those in which both your bodies are pointing in the same direction, but as long as your tongue can reach her vagina, then any position will do.

You must remember that tastes – literally and metaphorically – differ tremendously in this department. What may be a great oral sex technique for one individual may be totally inappropriate for another. In order to be a great oral aficionado, the secret is timing, listening and responding. Once again, it's all to do with communication. Take time to do oral sex, and do it sometimes without penetration in mind. Pay attention to your partner's moans and groans and her body movements to work out what is working for her and what isn't. Respond according to what is working, and keep doing it.

Make it apparent to your partner that you are enjoying yourself too. Oral sex is not something you just do to someone else: you are participating and sharing in the activity and relishing the intimacy, the effects you are having and, in fact, the entire experience.

1 Where to begin
Begin by kissing and sucking around the vulva, luxuriating in everything, excluding the clitoris. The clitoris is highly sensitive and needs plenty of forewarning before it is touched. Heading straight there can cause discomfort and, at times, even pain. Gently spread your partner's outer labia with your fingers and kiss and suck her inner labia in the same way that you would if you were kissing her passionately on the mouth. When you notice her starting to respond, glide your tongue between the folds of the inner labia. If her response is a sharp jerk or she pushes away from you, stay away from there for a while, concentrating instead on the outer edges and massaging her pubic mound with your hand.

2 Going for gold
Once your partner is sufficiently relaxed and turned on, you can expose the clitoral shaft, which runs down from the top of the labia to the clitoral head, underneath the inner labia. You may find it helps to spread the labia with two hands to make the skin taut, exposing the shaft. This area of densely packed nerve endings is extremely sensitive, and a soft-tongue/hard-tongue approach usually works best here. Try to stimulate it first with your tongue relaxed and soft, then, if she begins grinding towards you, you can

increase the pressure by tensing and firming your tongue muscles. Remember to keep your tongue well lubricated with saliva.

3 Different strokes
How you stimulate the clitoris is very individual to the woman. Some like a soft sucking or caressing action, while others prefer a harder and sharper flicking action, either up and down or sideways. Flicking it upwards (i.e. away from her vagina) is said to give a much greater sensation than downwards, but this is, of course, a matter of personal taste. If the clitoris enlarges, then she likes what you are doing; if it shrinks, then stop. However, remember that just before orgasm, the clitoris often retracts and seemingly disappears, so it is important to read other signs from her as well, otherwise you might stop just at the crucial moment.

4 The crab
Remember doing the crab in the gym, when you raised your arched body up, supporting yourself only with your feet and hands? Well this is a variation for the more supple lover. You sit, while the woman positions herself face up with her knees hooked over your shoulders and her head between your knees or legs. From here she arches her back and uses her hands on the floor to support herself, raising her genitals closer to your face.

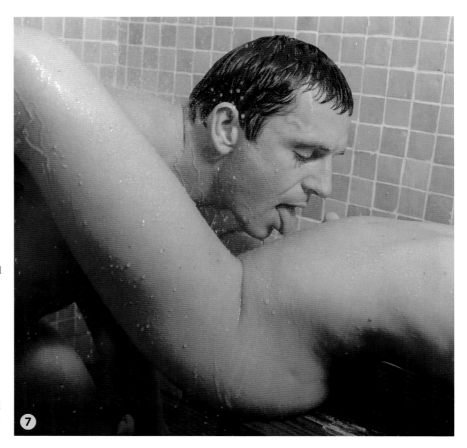

5 Spicing it up

Drinking hot and cold drinks before oral sex can lead to different sensations for your partner, but do be aware that the clitoral head is hypersensitive and may not necessarily respond well to extremes. Occasionally the head can become irritated, which will certainly cool down the proceedings and not make you flavour of the week.

Incorporating a vibrator can add to the experience; place it under your tongue, so the vibrations transmit through you.

To really extend playtime, bring her to the brink of orgasm and then stop for a good 30 seconds, bring her back to the brink then stop for less time, and so on. Some women may not appreciate this stop-go technique, so it's best to discuss it first.

6 Keep the rhythm going

When you can tell that your partner is just about to come, make sure you don't change a thing. Whatever you're doing is working, so just hold your ground and prepare for the tsunami. When she comes, don't necessarily stop, unless she asks you to, but lighten the touch slightly and perhaps take the emphasis away from the clitoris, which may now be hypersensitive. Continuing stimulation around the clitoris can increase the orgasm, and some women even report multiple orgasms from good oral sex.

7 Licking the clitoris

Imagine you're drawing small circles on and around her clitoris with your tongue. The smaller circles will concentrate on the tip and the larger ones will deal with the base. Alternate the speed and direction of the circles, as some women respond better if the circles rotate in a specific direction. You should be able to tell from her response which direction is her favourite.

Draw figures-of-eight over her clitoris with your tongue. This may be too much stimulation for some women, but for others it will work wonders. Experiment with the speed and frequency.

Use your tongue to flick the clitoris either up and down, with a short pause between each flick, or from left to right, aiming just underneath the base of the head. Vary the pressure of the flicks and their frequency.

8 The edge

Ask your partner to lie down on the bed, on her front or back, with her bottom over the edge of the bed. Kneel on the floor between her legs, hooking them over your shoulders. Placing your hands under her bottom or pelvis means that you can now raise her up or lower her down to achieve the perfect angle for you to start licking.

9 The triangle

If doing a headstand, or maybe some yoga, appeals to your partner, she'll like this position. Standing either on the bed or the floor, she should bend down, keeping her legs straight, until her head touches the surface (placing her hands on either side for balance). You then sit under this inverted V shape, with your head between her legs, so that the tops of her thighs are supported by your shoulders, and your legs stick straight out on either side of her head. Your mouth will now be in the perfect position for some genital massaging, and your hands are still free to massage anything else they can reach.

10 Face sitting

This position has two variations, both of which are equally enjoyable. Lie on your back and ask your partner to crouch or kneel over your face, facing your feet. As she nestles her bottom down on to your face, you get an erotically close-up view of her genitalia, before starting to work your magic. Alternatively, she can sit facing your head, which means that you get to see her breasts dangling above you, and she can watch you at work. This is a great position for women, as they can control the pressure by either easing off or grinding down. But mind you don't get suffocated in the throes of passion.

5 Divine inspiration

…Tantra involves raising the chakras and awakening kundalini, which means, of course, bigger and better orgasms…

Ancient erotica

Advance inspiration for your lovemaking is available in the form of ancient Chinese and Indian texts. Over the last 3,000 years, Eastern cultures have worshipped and respected the power and life force of human sexual nature. Although contemporary Western society is more liberal and open than in the past, the arts of seduction, sensuality and wanton abandon have been under-developed here by comparison. By looking towards the East, we can borrow wisdom and teachings from a long history of enlightened sexual revolutionaries.

There are several texts that have been translated in the West. Most famous is the *Kama Sutra*, a Hindu text not solely sexually focused; in fact, only a small portion of the text concentrates on the act of sex. It advises on aspects of male–female relations such as courtship and marriage, the duties of wife and husband and enhancing beauty and attractiveness, and it provides a variety of recipes and incantations to help with sexual problems and difficulties.

The *Ananga Ranga* was directed more at long-term couples, and aimed to relieve "the monotony which follows possession". The writer, Kalyana Malla, wrote a long treatise of erotic work, which incorporated the much older *Kama Sutra*, describing a multitude of kisses, embraces and sexual positions. Although originally written for a male readership, the *Ananga Ranga* seeks to help couples to renew their desire for sex, which, in turn, helps them to re-establish strong bonds, both of friendship and love.

More than a practice or step-by-step guide, Tantra is a philosophy concerned with spirituality and divine energy, blending sacred sexuality, Eastern philosophy and the teachings of the *Kama Sutra*. It involves the use of meditation and yoga to master the ultimate goal of dissipating the ego and creating union with the divine energy that is within each of us. Tantra involves raising the chakras and awakening kundalini, which means, of course, bigger and better orgasms.

Passionate violence
The *Kama Sutra* has only a short section on sexual positions, which, not unsurprisingly, is the part that is most notorious. Among the chapters suggesting how the eldest wife should conduct herself towards the younger wives of her husband, and how she should behave among courtesans, is a short section dedicated to the things a man can do to give a woman pleasure. It also goes into great detail about the passionate violence that sometimes accompanies love-making. This is not to advocate fighting in the bedroom, but it does acknowledge that some couples find that gently striking and biting each other during sexual congress is an expression of, and adds to, the excitement. Obviously, this type of behaviour works only if it is done by mutual agreement, but, if you both agree, then go ahead.

10 divine tips to drive her wild

While the *Kama Sutra* does include a list of exotic positions for sex, it also describes in great detail the delicacy of foreplay and the importance of both parties being satisfied sexually, and states that they should share time together as a couple after congress.

Foreplay is an essential part of all sexual encounters, since it helps to relax and acquaint the partners with each other's bodies and erogenous zones, allowing both to reach the same levels of excitement before actual penetration. Making sure that his partner is willing and desirous is deemed the role of the man. Taking this kind of time to note your partner's reactions would certainly help to remove any doubt in the matter.

1 The work of the man

In the *Kama Sutra*, the "work of the man" denotes any action that the man must do in order to give pleasure to the woman. The author, Vatsayana suggests that when a man and a woman first come together, they should begin by sitting on the bed talking about non-sexual topics and encouraging each other to drink wine. As the talking relaxes the couple and the wine loosens inhibitions, the woman may lie down on the man's bed. While she is lying there, engrossed by his captivating conversation, the man should loosen her undergarments and "overwhelm her" with kisses if she starts to protest.

When he becomes erect, it is suggested that he should begin gently touching her with his hands. If she is shy or it is the first time they have had sex together, he should begin by placing his hands between her thighs. He should also caress her breasts, neck and armpits with his hands.

The contemporary message of the concept of "the work of the man" is about the importance of foreplay. Take time to seduce each other in bed with words and actions and some good wine. Your partner does not have to be passive; you can both luxuriate in the sensuality of each other's body before actually having intercourse.

2 Satisfying a woman

During sex, the man should concentrate on pressing the parts of the woman's body "on which she turns her eyes". Signs that a woman is enjoying herself are that she will turn (roll or close) her eyes, will become less shy and will press herself towards him to keep their sex organs as closely united as possible. When the woman shakes her hands, prevents the man from getting up, bites or kicks him, or continues writhing after he has climaxed, it signifies that she is aroused and requires more satisfaction.

It is interesting that Indian culture was so aware of the sexual needs of women at a time when the Western world seemed completely oblivious of them. Male reading of the body movements of women during intercourse allows you both to remain at the same tempo. If you come before your partner and ignore her own need for sexual fulfilment, then you will invariably leave her feeling frustrated.

3 The end of congress

After sex, the two lovers must show modesty by not looking at each other and by going separately to the bathroom. They should eat betel leaves and the man should anoint the woman's body with sandalwood. He must then embrace her with his left arm and hold a cup in his other hand, from which he should encourage her to drink.

Together they should eat sweetmeats, soup, mango juice or lemon juice mixed with sugar, anything that is sweet and pure. The couple should then sit outside on a balcony and enjoy the moonlight, with her lying in his lap as they talk. As they gaze at the night sky, he should show her the different constellations of stars and planets.

Don't panic, most women today do not consider an astronomy lesson an essential post-coital activity, although if you do know a bit about stars and planets it can be romantic to share it. Following the above advice is actually a perfect way of spending time together after you have had sex. Enjoy these moments – share a drink, massage one another with scented oils, feed each other with confectionery or fruit, or have a light meal, before cuddling up together for a chat. Star gazing is optional.

4 Make love to 32 women

The *Ananga Ranga* differs from the *Kama Sutra* in recognizing that maintaining erotic interest in a long-term relationship is no easy task. The book defines the difference between intimacy and familiarity and encourages partners to break down patterns of laziness. Kalyana Malla wrote: "Fully understanding the way in which such quarrels arise, I have in this book shown how the husband, by varying the enjoyment of his wife, may live with her as with thirty-two different women, ever varying the enjoyment of her, and rendering satiety impossible." Thus, boredom is relieved, and harmony returns to the breakfast table.

5 Mouth congress

Cunnilingus doesn't get much of a write-up in the ancient texts – it was considered just another form of kissing. However, these few ideas make enlightened reading.

jihva-bhramanaka – the circling tongue
The man uses his nose to spread the woman's vaginal lips and then gently probes her *yoni* (genitals) with his tongue. Then, with his nose, lips and chin, he moves in gentle circles all around her vaginal area, massaging her in three places at once.

chushita – sucked. The man fastens his lips to the woman's vaginal lips (labia) and nibbles at her before sucking on her clitoris.

He uses varying degrees of pressure as he sucks on her clitoris until he finds one that she is most comfortable with and, more importantly, one that gives her pleasure.

uchchushita – sucked up. The man cups and lifts his partner's buttocks, and uses his tongue to massage her navel, working down to her genitals.

6 The power of a kiss

Kissing and erotic massage are given great importance in all of the ancient texts. It was recognized that foreplay and touch were very important to the satisfaction of the female party, especially the different

techniques of kissing. In *ghatika* kissing, the man covers his partner's eyes with his hands and closes his own eyes before thrusting his tongue into his partner's mouth, moving it to and fro using a slow, pleasant motion that suggests another form of enjoyment.

By removing one sense, in this case sight, the partners' bodies become more attuned to other sensations. In this case, sex is simulated with the mouth, building anticipation about how each will pleasure the other genitally. It is a provocative yet romantic method of kissing, ideal as a precursory invitation to a night of sensational sexual activity.

7 Scratching

Both the *Ananga Ranga* and the *Kama Sutra* suggest that scratching should be tried only when love becomes intense. Nails should be clean, and both parties must be willing to try this before either of you commences.

Traditionally, marks or scratches are made by your first three fingers on the woman's back, breasts or genitals. It is most commonly done as a token of remembrance before the man leaves to go abroad. Parts of the body, such as the thighs and buttocks, can withstand more pain than the more sensitive areas around the face. They also have the advantage of being hidden by clothing.

8 Biting

Biting each other is a common outlet of sexual energy when in the throes of orgasm, and many people, both male and female, claim that they have been surprised afterwards at the depth of a bite. Many people enjoy sharp pain at the height of passion to enhance the powerful shudders of pleasure that they experience during orgasm.

Bindhu-dashana is the mark left by the man's two front teeth on the woman's lower lip. The lower lip is very supple and elastic, and gentle sucking and nibbling on it is very pleasurable. In the days when the *Ananga Ranga* was written, it was probably pretty

acceptable for women to bear the marks of their husband's desire. Any imprint of passion today is reminiscent of the adolescent love bite, and should be avoided.

9 Stroking

Softly fondling the hair of a woman, states the *Ananga Ranga*, is a good method of kindling a lasting desire.

Samahastakakeshagrahana – stroking the hair. The man strokes his partner's hair between the palms of his hands, at the same time kissing her with passion. Gentle pulling and playing with a woman's hair is very erotic and sensual. When pulling hair, make sure you get a good handful, as pulling at just a few hairs can be very painful. Why not take this a stage further and gently pull tufts of each other's pubic hair?

10 Hair pulling

Kamavatansakeshagrahana – pulling the hair. This is done during sexual intercourse, when each partner grabs the other's hair above the ears as they kiss passionately. This type of hair pulling is ideal in the throes of passion, when the body's touch sensors are dulled by the other erotic sensations that are flowing around. Stroking and massaging this area, including the temples, is very seductive, especially if you whisper in each other's ears.

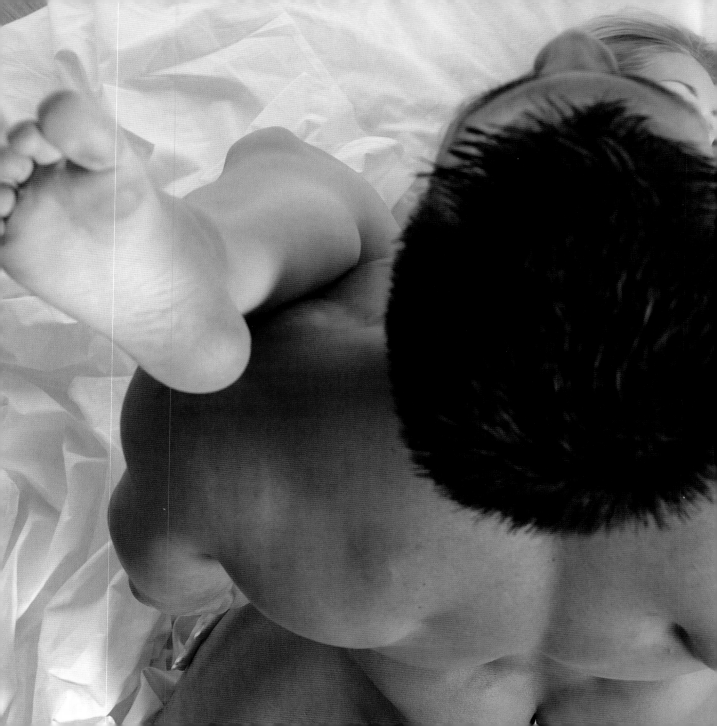

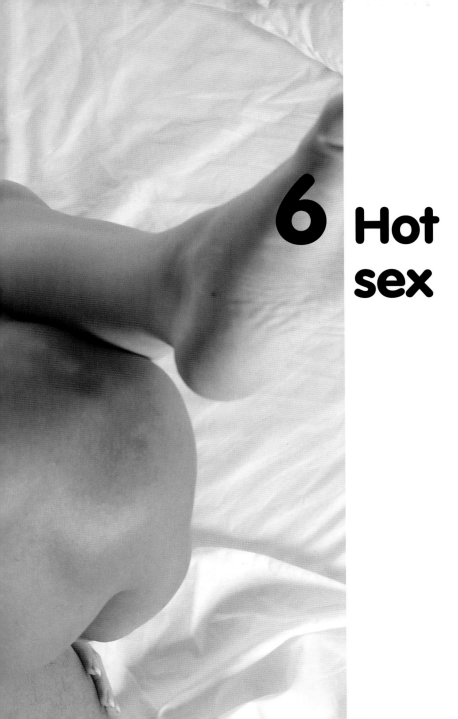

6 Hot sex

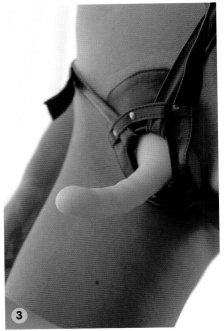

10 tips for hot sex

You wouldn't go and see the same film every week, so why keep doing the same things in bed? After a while, doing the same thing over and over again can feel too safe, and, yes, boring. To keep things interesting, it is crucial to try something new once in a while. It may not become a favourite straightaway, but hopefully you will both have had some fun in the process, and there is always something else to try the next time.

1 Erotica
Most women are a little ambivalent about erotica. You may be used to those magazines you keep under the bed, but most women don't get off on looking at pornography. You can see their point. Most of it depicts images of women looking rather vulnerable and coy with no clothes on, usually to the detriment of someone's dignity – not exactly a turn-on for your average heterosexual girl. However, there are degrees of depravity. Women might prefer to read about sex rather than see it, and then they can make up visual images that suit themselves. Invite your partner to choose a raunchy book, then read it to her as part of your foreplay.

2 Anal sex
Practising anal sex is a tighter and more intense experience for both of you. If it is done correctly and carefully, the vaginal and rectal walls can swell during arousal, giving her extra pleasure. She may need convincing, at first, that this is worth trying, and make sure you are prepared to stop at any stage if she changes her mind. It is worth mentioning that many people, both men and women, find anal sex a hugely enjoyable experience. The difference between anal pain and pleasure is relaxation, and the key is to use plenty of lubrication and to take it very slowly.

3 Strap-on pleasure
If your partner develops a taste for anal sex, she might even enjoy practising it on you, so why not buy her a strap-on dildo? It will also give her the chance to play the penetrator for once, which could be quite liberating for her. It could even become a regular feature of your lovemaking. From your point of view, you'll not only get the chance of having your G spot (your prostate gland) stimulated, but you'll also know how it feels to be on the receiving end for once.

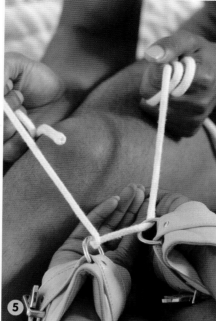

4 Role play

All of us have sexual fantasies, and there is nothing so exciting as acting them out. Your partner may be worried that you will think she's some sex-crazed maniac if she shows even the slightest desire to dress up in something raunchy (and she could be right). Start by talking about it, then maybe take it in turns to dress up for each other. She might get just as much excitement from dressing up as a buxom barmaid or a leather-encased catwoman as you do from watching her. When it's your turn, wear whatever outfit she's chosen for you, and do your best to fulfil her fantasy – whatever it is.

5 Tie me down

Some women have difficulty achieving orgasm with penetrative sex and find that a little light bondage resolves the problem. If their problem is a psychological one, then being restrained takes the guilt away: if they cannot resist, then it is out of their hands, so they can just lie back and enjoy the whole sensual experience.

You don't have to get too serious about bondage to enjoy the frisson of losing, or taking, complete control. We're not talking about sinister black masks, chains and long whips here, more a case of fabric handcuffs.

Bondage can be described as any sexual act that involves restraint, and it is important that it is consensual. There must always be an agreed "release word", so that if either of you wants to stop, saying this word will get the message across. (Just using "stop" doesn't always work, because yelling this at the top of her voice could be part of your partner's enjoyment of the whole bondage experience.)

6 Spanking

Some men and women simply enjoy the odd thump on the rump – either giving or receiving it – and if it's combined with a bit of role play, then so much the better. Do remember to keep within previously agreed boundaries to prevent either of you from getting unintentionally hurt. In the heat of the moment, one of you may forget your own strength. Begin slowly and gently with a light slap or two and then, if you want, increase the pressure in response to your partner. Keep it light-hearted and fun, and make sure you give as good as you get.

7

9

There are two advantages of this from your partner's viewpoint. First, you can delay your own orgasm until you can sense that she is ready. Then you can climax in glorious unison. Second, if she's feeling particularly randy, you'll be ready to go again pretty quickly, instead of lying there exhausted and starting to snore.

When many men feel that they are about to come, they hold their breath, as if forcing the orgasm to come out. In *maithuna*, however, you keep your breathing regular, and put the tip of your tongue on the roof of your mouth and roll it into a "straw" to breathe through. Concentrate by focusing on your third-eye. This can help to circulate the energy and delay the orgasm – although it may be best to warn her in advance.

7 Doing it together

Watching you masturbate is probably not your partner's idea of a good night in, but if you masturbate together, you can have the enjoyment of watching one another come – maybe even at the same time, if you're clever. Your partner may enjoy masturbating in front of you, perhaps doing it rather coyly at first with her underwear still on to make it a tantalizing, rather than graphic, experience.

8 A bit of fun

Lots of women might find your rendition of *The Full Monty* dance a laugh. Give your partner a surprise by performing your own style of striptease. Put on some suitable music, and, while she is sitting comfortably, you can gyrate for her, slowly and tantalizingly removing one piece of clothing at a time. If you have the hat for the job too, then all the better.

9 Massage

A massage is one of the most enjoyable ways to approach a night of passion. She may have had a long day, so suggest a gentle massage to help her unwind. Have some fluffy towels for her to lie on, some candles burning and soft music playing. Next thing you know, she is relaxed, you are touching each other intimately, and if the mood is right, one thing will lead to another. Invest in some mild massage oil – almond oil is generally non-allergenic – and be sure to warm it in your hands before you begin.

10 Sexual yoga

The Tantric skill of *maithuna* is a technique for controlling response, designed to help delay and intensify male orgasm. The technique is designed to help the flow of sexual energy and to ensure that you feel energized after sex as opposed to exhausted.

10

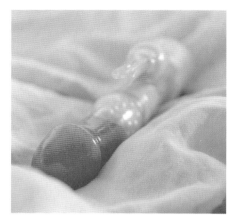

Hot toys

Sex toys have become *de rigueur* as the face of sexual awareness has changed. There are so many toys to choose from, in all sorts of shapes, colours and sizes. Aesthetics are as important as function, and nowadays sex toys are becoming desirable designer items. And they're not just for women. There are as many gizmos and gadgets for men, from anal beads to penis rings. We are becoming more open to the idea of incorporating toys into sex play. Sex toys have the advantage of spicing it up between the sheets, and should give both of you some fun as you experiment.

Vibrators

It's easy to confuse a vibrator with a dildo, so what is the difference? Well, the vibrator vibrates and the dildo doesn't. They differ in shape, too. Vibrators are used more for genital massage and are not necessarily phallic in shape. In fact, these days they can be pretty well any shape, as the pictures above and below right show. Dildos, however, are shaped like penises and are designed more for anal or vaginal penetrative use.

The advantage of the vibrator for women is that those who need constant clitoral stimulation to achieve orgasm can incorporate it into their lovemaking. They can also use it for an all-over body massage, starting at the top and working down. Some women find the vibrator more effective than the hand, tongue or penis.

Remember to keep a supply of batteries handy, as there are few things worse than a pre-orgasmic power failure.

Dildos

Like vibrators, dildos are made in a variety of different shapes, sizes, colours and textures, but they are associated with penetration rather than massage. They are usually phallic in shape, but this can vary from a lifelike penis (often complete with testicles) to a simple cylindrical structure.

Dildos have a history that stretches back 30,000 years, so if you're feeling a bit embarrassed about buying one, remember you are by no means the first.

When buying a dildo intended for anal penetration, make sure that it has a flared end to prevent it disappearing up the rectum. You will thus be spared an embarrassing emergency trip to the local hospital. If you use a dildo for anal penetration, be sure to use a condom and dispose of it once you are finished, as the anus harbours many bacteria that could cause infection if the dildo is then used for vaginal penetration.

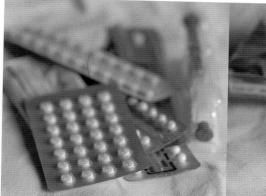

Love balls

These are two weighted balls of about 3cm/1¼in in diameter, though sometimes smaller, which are placed inside the vagina. The weights rock and jiggle together as you move around, causing the balls to shift. One advantage of them is that they help you with your pelvic floor exercises. They are also fairly discreet and can be worn anywhere. Some women love them and report fantastic orgasms while waiting for the bus, others say they can't feel a thing.

Lubrication

The production of love juice is not always directly related to arousal. In fact, it is hormone-controlled and its presence or absence can depend on a host of things from certain times in the menstrual cycle, the effects of childbirth and hysterectomy to the drying effects of alcohol and marijuana. Be sure to have some lubrication to hand, as drying up can often be the kiss of death to a steamy sex session.

Some of the properties in commercial sexual lubricants kill sperm, so avoid them if you are trying to have a baby. Lubrication is an essential component in anal play, as the anus and surrounding area produce no lubrication. Use water-based lubricants if you are using sex toys or condoms.

Safer sex

Contraception is for everyone, whether male, female, married or single. When you are in a relationship, contraception should be seen as a mutual project and not the responsibility of the woman alone. It is not just about getting pregnant, there are countless sexually transmitted infections (STIs) you can catch. You should also remember that no contraceptive is 100 per cent effective, though many are close. For extra peace of mind you can always use more than one product – such as the contraceptive pill combined with condoms.

Hormonal methods

The contraceptive pill is hormone-controlled contraception for women, which is either in the form of the combined pill or the progesterone-only pill. For longer-acting contraception, an injection is now available that is 99 per cent effective. It slowly releases progesterone into the body, preventing ovulation. Each injection lasts for 8–12 weeks. Implanon is a progesterone implant that acts in a similar way by releasing progesterone into the body. It is 99 per cent effective and lasts for three years, but can lead to irregular periods or even cause them to stop altogether. Hormonal methods do not provide protection against STIs, so should be used with a barrier method.

In addition to the female pill, new male contraceptives are under development in the form of a transdermal gel and patch that rely on MENT™ (7a-methyl-19-nortestosterone), a synthetic steroid that resembles testosterone but without the unwanted side effect of an enlarged prostate.

Barrier methods

Condoms are the most common forms of barrier method. If used properly they are 94–98 per cent effective, but always make sure they carry an official approval symbol. Condoms should be put on as soon as the penis is erect because it can drip semen before ejaculation. Although robust, they must be used with care as they can split or come off. You must withdraw as soon as you ejaculate and make sure that you do not spill any semen. It is important to use extra-strong condoms when performing anal sex, to allow for the greater pressure caused by the tightness of the anus, as well as to protect against any STIs. In addition, anal sex without a condom can result in faecal matter and bacteria becoming trapped in your urethral opening, which may not be removed by washing. This can lead to infections in you, and also in your partner if vaginal penetration should follow anal sex.

Index